Frontispiece. A. *A bend in the lower Purgatoire River.* **B.** *Large rock from Southeast Colorado with many Pecked Pictorial style petroglyphs.*

Petroglyphs

of Southeast Colorado and the Oklahoma Panhandle

by
Bill McGlone
Ted Barker
Phil Leonard

Library of Congress Card Number: 94-76663

ISBN: 0-9641333-0-X

Published by Mithras, Inc.
3520 N. SR–32
Kamas, UT 84036

Printed in the United State of America
Publishers Press
Salt Lake City, UT

CONTENTS

FOREWORD

Longstanding curiosity about unorthodox interpretations of petro-glyphs in the neighborhood of the Purgatoire River led me at last to con-tact Bill McGlone about arranging a visit, in July, 1993, to a few of the more-publicized sites. Although I have visited more than 1200 ancient and prehistoric sites and monuments throughout the world, southeast Colorado and the Oklahoma Panhandle might as well have been the moon. I had never been there. I didn't know what it was like. The land and its rock art weren't described much in books, except for those co-authored by Bill McGlone, Phil Leonard, and others. I assumed that places like Sun Temple, Anubis Cave, and Crack Cave were aberrations of rocky outcrops in what must otherwise be just more Great Plains. My geographical naiveté was only exceeded by my ignorance of the remarkable archaeolog-ical resources of the area.

La Junta, Colorado, is the modern trailhead for the places studied by the authors of this book. History converges in La Junta. It was the junction of the old Navajo and Santa Fe trails. It played, therefore, an important part in the settlement and development of the West. U.S. 50 connects La Junta with the eastern flank of the Rockies along a route that parallels the railroad and is unrelieved by topographical novelty. It's a good place to ranch, farm, and run freight, and that's what a fair number of people do there. It doesn't qualify as one of America's scenic wonderlands. Scenic wonderland is hidden, however, in the rolling grasslands reached from La Junta.

As we drove out of La Junta, Bill McGlone started pointing out to me surprises in the landscape—mesas, unexpected rock formations, rock art panels, zones with prehistoric remains, stones placed upright by people of the thousand-year-old Apishipa Focus, places linked with Spanish entradas and with skirmishes between Plains Indians and the U.S. Cavalry, and the deep and stunning canyons of the Purgatoire drainage.

The territory's past is rich, complex, and relatively unstudied. The rock art possesses bewildering variety, and hardly anyone writes about it. Most of the recent reports are concerned with what the authors here have called the "Ogam Corridor." Controversial claims concerning Old World visitors and archaeoastronomy have directed attention to the region, but most of its rock art has never been described or recorded. Sherman Lawton published a short paper on rock art in the Oklahoma Panhandle in 1962, and it is referenced in Klaus F. Wellmann's comprehensive book, *A Survey of North American Indian Rock Art*. Wellmann, however, passed along little detail and no pictures. You can track down a handful of specialist research papers on the rock art of southeast Colorado, but documentation is sparse. We can understand this lapse, however. Colorado is the state with nationally registered cliff dwellings and world-class ski resorts. The petroglyphs in the canyons of the Arkansas River and two of its tributaries—the Purgatoire and the Cimarron—have gotten lost in the shuffle . . . until now.

Lucky to be traveling through the canyons and grasslands with a team of guides that included Bill McGlone, ranchers Alma and Ted Barker, and retired ranchers Margaret and Earl Goodrich, I realized they had the kind of detailed local knowledge and experience that a published study of the region's rock art would require. Ted Barker and Bill McGlone took the suggestion, and with Phil Leonard they ran with it. There is a lot of rock art in their territory, and this book is the first comprehensive survey of what until now has been *piedra incognita*. The marvels that follow confirm that there are still plenty of surprises left by the past and many lessons to be learned on the Purgatoire.

E.C. Krupp, Ph.D.,
Director,
Griffith Observatory,
Los Angeles, CA.

INTRODUCTION

Books have been written on the petroglyphs of most of the states west of the Mississippi River, but no summary of the petroglyphs of southeast Colorado and the Oklahoma Panhandle has been prepared. The region between the Arkansas and Cimarron rivers from the Rockies to Kansas may seem an unlikely place for people to have carved and painted rocks, and most rock art enthusiasts are unaware of what is there. That is indeed unfortunate because the area has an abundance of unusually varied and interesting petroglyphs.

We have prepared this book to fill that void. It is not intended to be a definitive study of the petroglyphs of the region; rather, it is an overview of what is present, using simplified classifications of style and chronology. Our primary purpose is to show the extensive number and many types of glyphs in this rather limited and isolated region and to interest specialists in their study. We also want to help the people of Colorado become aware of an important and easily overlooked aspect of their heritage.

The petroglyphs described occur in an unusual stylistic mix, ranging in size from deer only a few inches long to a life-size buffalo and ranging from over four millennia to a few years in age. Techniques of pecking, boring, incising, abrading, rubbing, and painting have been used to make the glyphs. Most of the sites are on private land, inaccessible to the public, and can be seen only in books such as this, but some are on public land where they can be visited by all. We have not indicated the location of non-public sites in order to protect the privacy of the owners, and request readers' cooperation in respecting that privacy. Petroglyphs today are subject to increasing destructive pressures from the environment and undisciplined public contact. Viewing petroglyphs at appropriately protected sites is in order, but visitors should avoid any physical contact with the glyphs to conserve them and their settings.

Publishing a book such as this generates mixed emotions. Does one put the petroglyphs at some risk of vandalism by describing their existence? Or, is this offset by the right of people to know details of the history of this country? The consensus seems to be in favor of public knowledge, as many books have been written describing the petroglyphs of other regions. And, the opinions of colleagues and other interested people we consulted were almost unanimously in favor of publication, provided that locations were not specifically identified. Our concurrence with that view has resulted in this book.

The term *petroglyphs* is normally used to mean rock engravings while *pictographs* is the term used for rock paintings. *Petroglyphs* can also be used to mean the two collectively, as in our title. The authors have studied petroglyphs over much of the West for years, concentrating a large portion of their efforts in the region covered by the book. One of the authors, Ted Barker, has lived in southeast Colorado all his life, and another, Bill McGlone, now resides there. In addition to recording the regional petroglyphs shown here, we have evaluated the idea that some of the glyphs are ancient writing as found in the Old World. These epigraphic hypotheses are mentioned only briefly in the text. See McGlone et al. (1993) for details.

Some photos in the book show petroglyphs enhanced with aluminum powder, a practice formerly used by several investigators. Today, this is no longer done, as many researchers believe petroglyphs and their rock backgrounds should not be touched by anything, including tracing materials. Recording of petroglyphs is now done principally by photography and sketching (Appendix). Previous attempts to classify regional petroglyphs by style have been made by researchers, but we do not consider this work well enough established to follow it completely. The simplified categories we use are explained in the second chapter. The data for this book were collected as a by-product of our epigraphic investigations. As a result, our illustrations do not contain some reference details. There are no color or length indicators and relative size is not maintained.

The book is organized into chapters that give first the background to the subject in the form of descriptions of the region and style classifications of the petroglyphs found there. This is followed by chapters devoted to the various styles in chronological order, with all painted material described in one chapter, regardless of style or age. Finally , the subject of astronomically associated petroglyphs is covered, and a description of public sites is presented. The recording of petroglyphs is discussed in an appendix to help visitors who would like to retain in an acceptable way images of petroglyphs they see.

Some of the most interesting petroglyphs of the region are presented here, but there are many more that might have been included. Readers are encouraged to contact us about material we may not have seen or about information they may have concerning the history of some of the glyphs for inclusion in future editions of the book.

ACKNOWLEDGMENTS

The authors are indebted to a number of people for their assistance in the preparation of this book. We greatly appreciate Alma Barker's active participation in the writing of the book and in gathering the data for it. We would also like to thank Pete Faris, Phil Garn, Earl and Margaret Goodrich, Jim Guthrie, Rollin Gillespie, Al Kane, Greg McGlone, Judy Morehouse, John and Daphne Rudolph, Susan Touchstone, Truman and Leona Tucker, Don and Marita Vickroy, Jim Whittall, Mark Widing, the many reviewers of the manuscript, and those who supplied illustrations. In particular, we would like to thank Dr. Ed Krupp for his suggestion that this book be written and for writing the foreword. We are especially grateful to the many landowners who have let us explore their land to record the petroglyphs, but who cannot be named here. Illustrations are the work of the authors, except as otherwise noted.

CHAPTER 1

THE REGION

Southeast Colorado is often perceived as an extension of the plains of western Kansas, but driving south of the Arkansas River on Colorado highway 101 or 109, one is surprised to encounter the Cedar Breaks region, containing a number of inviting canyons along tributaries of the Arkansas and Cimarron Rivers. Most prominent is that cut through the Chaquaqua Plateau by the Purgatoire River (pronounced PURG-A-TORY), but called the "Picketwire" by natives probably as a corruption of the French pronunciation (PURG-A-TWAR). The main canyon is some four miles wide and 900 feet deep in one place. It extends for many miles and has numerous side canyons with walls 300 to 400 feet high. The canyons of the streams farther east are much shallower, with walls typically 50 to 100 feet high.

It is in these canyons, with streams flowing northeast toward the Arkansas and southeast toward the Cimarron, that the numerous petroglyphs and pictographs of this book are found. Some are on sheer caprock faces of the canyon walls, while others are on boulders strewn along stream beds. The glyphs are often concentrated at major sites that have several panels, and they occur in a variety of styles spanning a period of more than 4000 years.

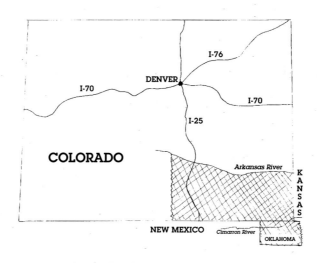

Region discussed in this book is shown in shaded area.

The region covered here is from the Arkansas River in the north to the Cimarron River in the south, except for one site in the Oklahoma Panhandle located in the North Canadian River drainage and two in the foothills of the Rockies. The primary region is only about 80 by 100 miles and is remarkable for its concentration and variety of petroglyphs. It is roughly the size of Massachusetts, but the portion where the petroglyphs are found is restricted to the even smaller area occupied by the streams and canyons. The accompanying map shows the portions of Colorado and Oklahoma discussed in this book.

Perhaps the presence of so many petroglyphs is not too surprising, because the canyons along the many streams have proved to be as inviting to early aboriginal peoples as to more recent sheepherders and cattle ranchers. The water has made irrigated agriculture possible for almost 2000 years, and wild game,such as bear, bison, antelope, deer, rabbits, squirrels, mountain lions, and even elk have lived here. Rolling fields of grass and wildflowers abound, and the brilliant blooming of the cholla cactus in June is a highlight of the year. Numerous sets of dinosaur tracks are also present in layers of sandstone uncovered by erosion caused by streams. Today, the land is either held in private ranches or is part of the Comanche National Grasslands and the newly established Picket Wire Canyonlands, both administered by the U.S. Forest Service. The private ranches are closed to the general public, but six major areas are on public land where the glyphs can be viewed. They are accessible as described in Chapter 10.

Many peoples have lived in the region, and most have left a petroglyphic record of their presence. Occupation began before the time of the people of the so-called Middle Archaic Period (3000 B.C. to 1000 B.C.), who were followed by the Late Archaic Period people (1000 B.C. to 1 A.D.). The Apishipa Focus people, who have no known modern descendants, lived here from about 800–1200 A.D. Then came the Plains Indians: first, the Apache possibly as early as 1350 A.D., followed by the Comanche and Cheyenne, with occasional incursions by Arapahoe, Ute, and Kiowa. Finally, the Europeans arrived: conquistadors, sheepherders, cowboys, the U. S. Cavalry, homesteaders, and farmers. The canyons have been home to many, and all have welcomed the refuge they offer from the uninviting continuity of the plains.

Artifacts show the presence of people who have lived in the region, yet only a few detailed archaeological studies have been conducted. Some Archaic arrow points have been found, along with many points left by more recent native inhabitants. There are the intriguing structural remains of the Apishipa Focus people that are usually thought to be house bases. Most often they are circles of standing stones made from two to three-foot-high slabs of sandstone set on edge. Some are circles in tangentially arranged groups of more than thirty. Many are set on promontories against sheer drop-offs with low protective walls inland, and some have much larger stones several feet long, usually set on end but sometimes laid log-like. A number of explanations have been offered, but the consensus is that most were domiciles, although a few do seem to suggest other purposes, such as ritual sites.

Later people left their artifacts, too: tepee rings of the nomadic Plains Indians; weapons and armor from early Spanish incursions; ruins of houses, post offices, churches, hotels, and stage stations by the settlers; rock cairns or "torreones," possibly used as territorial markers; cartridge cases from cavalry firefights with the Indians; and stone walls with a variety of purposes. One particularly enigmatic type of artifact is the so-called "stepping stone trail" of which there are numerous examples. These trails are composed of flat stones set in the ground about a stride apart, and some of them apparently run for miles. There are also reports of large geoglyphs, a possible medicine wheel, a buffalo jump, and Indian irrigation systems.

All in all, southeast Colorado is a fascinating and relatively unstudied area. Most interesting to us is its profusion of intriguing petroglyphs.

Animals that have lived in the region: antelope, deer, bison, and rattlesnake.

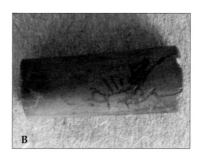

Inscribed bone artifacts from Bob Seaman's collection. **A:** Rib bone seven inches long from near the Arkansas River.
B, C: From a cave in the caprock of a side canyon in the upper Purgatoire River drainage from which the Spanish Peaks can be seen.
B: Hollow bone bead 5/8-inch long.
C: 1-3/4-inch long.

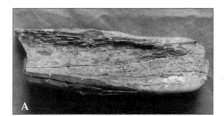

Artifacts found in the region. **A:** Tip of bone flesher found at depth of one foot in the center of the Apishipa Focus stone circle illustrated on page 6. **B:** Set of percussion-flaked stone tools of Alibates flint found together on the surface by Margaret Goodrich.

Metates rubbed into bedrock by Indians grinding corn or other materials.

Apishipa Focus stone circles made from slabs of sandstone, conventionally interpreted as house bases. The bone tool illustrated on page 5 was found by a rancher in the hole within the circle, shown at **A***. No further digging has been done, awaiting future professional excavation.*

Flowers of the region.
A: *Cholla cactus at left.*
Photo by Judy Morehouse.
B: *Yucca or soapweed.*
Photo by Marita Vickroy.

Unusual geologic formations from the region.
A: *Large "Pedestal Arch."*
B: *"Throne Rock."*

Stone cairns or "torreones," usually found on high points. They may have served as some type of territorial marker.

Petroglyphs are often found in difficult-to-reach places.

Remains of home-steaders' houses similar to these are found across the entire region.
A: *Author Ted Barker and his wife Alma in front of house in which they lived immediately after their marriage in 1941.*

Interesting man-made rock emplacements.
A: *Long rock wall or fence.*
B: *Large man-placed rock thought to be a spring marker.*
C: *Alma Barker standing in rock circle believed to be a tepee ring in which rocks were used to hold down walls of a tepee.*

Dinosaur tracks of the region. **A:** *Portion of extensive trackway in Picket Wire Canyonlands, now administered by the U.S. Forest Service. Photo by Marita Vickroy.* **B:** *Tracks near Kenton, Oklahoma. Truman Tucker and wife Leona in background.* **C:** *Photo by Judy Morehouse.*

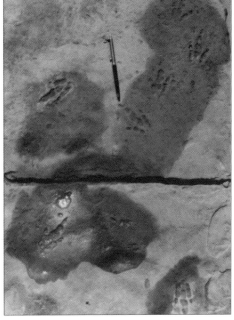

CHAPTER 2

STYLES AND CHRONOLOGY

Petroglyphs from different regions often look quite different, yet there may be sufficient commonality among the glyphs of one region that they can be described as being made in a single "style." Petroglyphic style can be thought of as the presence of recurring motifs with similar features or artistic expression that are usually engraved by the same technique, such as pecking or abrading. The Classic Vernal Fremont style of Utah, for example, is characterized by figures of people with trapezoidal bodies, "bucket" heads, and elaborate necklaces.

Attempts have been made to define styles for some of the petroglyphs in the southeast Colorado region. The most recent is that of Sally

Professor Ronald Dorn of Arizona State University taking a sample of rock varnish from grooves of a Plains Biographic petroglyph for radiocarbon determination of its age. A few grains of varnish from the bottom of the grooves is all that is needed.

Cole, followed by the work of Lawrence Loendorf. They proposed that the petroglyphs be classified as Pecked Abstract (including Pecked Curvilinear and Pecked Rectilinear similar to Great Basin Abstract), Pecked Representational, Pecked Purgatoire, Rio Grande, and Plains Biographic. These breakdowns are not yet well accepted, as they are based on only a small number of sites. We accept the classification of Pecked Abstract, but group the next three as Pecked Pictorial for the broad-view purpose of this book. "Pecked Pictorial" is sufficient here because these glyphs are pecked and do picture natural objects such as animals and people. We also accept the term "Plains Biographic" for the regional carvings of the Plains Indians.

In addition, we have included a chapter entitled "Parallel Lines," since groups of such lines are so common. We also include a chapter on pictographs in which we make no attempt to separate them into styles. New techniques now available for dating painted material should make more detailed classification of the pictographs possible in the near future.

Dating of petroglyphs has been accomplished in the past by association of stylistic elements with art forms of known age such as pottery designs, or by uncovering glyphs from dated archaeological strata. Techniques for dating the petroglyph grooves by radiocarbon methods have recently been developed by Professor Ronald Dorn of Arizona State University. This is possible because the patina or rock varnish that forms very slowly on rocks in the dry climate of the western United States contains organic matter whose age can be measured by radiocarbon dating. The varnish is quite thin, and thus the carving of grooves exposes virgin rock. The subsequent varnish formation in the grooves becomes an indicator of their age. The varnish is very hard and protects the grooves from the erosive action of the elements. See McGlone et al. (1993, Appendix B) for a more detailed description.

Working with the authors and later with Loendorf, Dorn has dated a number of the petroglyphs of the southeast Colorado region. A summary and interpretation of the results of these tests is currently being prepared by Peter Faris and is planned for publication in 1994. This work dates the Pecked Abstract style from the third millennium B.C. to the first millennium A.D., and the Plains Biographic can be placed in the past 100 to 500 years. The Pecked Pictorial group of styles falls between the other two in age and somewhat overlaps each. The Historic European material is mostly from the last 300 years or so, and often contains dates as part of inscriptions. See the following Table for a summary of the styles and their dating. Statistical treatment of the dating data will be presented in Faris's paper.

There is, then, a tradition of petroglyph engraving in southeast Colorado over the last 4700 years in a sequence of styles that ends with modern graffiti.

REGION STYLE TYPES			
Pecked Abstract	Pecked Pictorial	Plains Biographic	Historic European
2700 B.C. to 850 A.D.	1350 B.C. to 1650 A.D.	1500 A.D. to Present	1541 A.D. to Present
			Santa Fe Trail Autographs Cowboy art
Parellel Lines (1000 B.C. to Present)			

Dates given are ranges of averages of three tests on individual petroglyphs. A total of 23 Pecked Abstract, 42 Pecked Pictorial, 4 Plains Biographic, and 5 Parallel Line glyphs were tested.

CHAPTER 3

PECKED ABSTRACT

The Pecked Abstract style, as the name implies, is not pictorial, but abstract in form. It contains a number of stylistic elements that some day may be the basis for further subdivision into useful substyles. Pecked meanders, grids, riverine-looking lines, map-like sequences, and so-called "pretzels" all occur alone or together. Several of these elements and combinations of them are found in the Great Basin Abstract style of Utah, Nevada, California, and Arizona.

Geometric signs are also found carved in a similar manner at site after site: in lines, in columns, and individually. They also occur in combination with the meanders, grids, etc. These signs show a remarkable correspondence to letters of the North Arabian alphabets, Thamudic and Safaitic. Arabian scholars have tried to read them without success, but think they may be writing and have encouraged further study of their possible connection to the Old World. These signs have been dated from 1900 to 2300 years old, the time of the use of the Thamudic and Safaitic alphabets in Arabia. See McGlone et al. (1993, Chapter 13) for further details.

Other Pecked Abstract style motifs are based on these geometric signs in the form of ligatures (combinations) of them that produce more elaborate symbols. A ⚲ and a — can be combined to produce ⚲ , for example. Finally, the phi-like sign ⚲ , is present in numerous variations, such as ⚲ , ⚲ , ⊕ , and ⚲ , all of which also occur in Arabia. The phi-like symbol is believed by the authors to be associated with hunting or hunting success because some appear like arrows in animals' backs. Other interpretations are that they may represent atlatls, fertility symbols, or water signs.

The Pecked Abstract glyphs are always made by pecking out the lines (grooves) that form them. This often appears to have been carefully done in a manner that sometimes yields fairly thin lines and shows the use of a fine-pointed tool. To date, we have been unable to reproduce this workmanship in our own experiments or to determine the specific type of tool that was used. It has also been suggested that some of the glyphs may have been made by boring rather than pecking.

The petroglyphs of this style are usually very dark from repatination and therefore are often quite difficult to see unless the lighting is correct. At one major site, a large panel was clearly revealed by sunlight just after noon in June. We had previously visited the site more than 30 times without seeing many details of the panel. This selective lighting effect can be simulated for recording, using a video light as described in Appendix A. A few glyphs have been repecked by later peoples. This is apparent from their fresher appearance and the presence of old, heavily patinated peck marks in the bottom of the grooves.

Pecked Abstract panel whose details were unknown until revealed by low angle sunlight in June.

The ubiquity of the Pecked Abstract style glyphs across the region is surprising, as they are found scattered along virtually every stream. These glyphs are usually pecked on boulders, along canyon floors, or on benches well below the rimrock; but occasionally, they are found on caprock faces or on top of the caprock just back from a canyon's rim. The people who made these glyphs visited almost every canyon, side canyon, and spring, leaving petroglyphic evidence of their passage. Some of the glyphs occur in sequences that suggest trail markers, others seem to mark the entrances to canyons, and still others have the appearance of maps, although none of these inferences can be drawn with any degree of certainty today.

Sometimes the glyphs occur in concentrations at large sites that have many panels. Although surface remains of domiciles at these major sites are rare, we recommend archaeological investigation at selected sites for further understanding of who pecked the petroglyphs. Further attempts to break this style into substyles should also help increase our understanding of these people.

"The Blackboard Rock."
A: *View of site.*
B: *Detail of face.*

Various Pecked Abstract petroglyphs.
A: *On short monolith. Photo by Jim Whittall.*
B: *Michelle McFarlane beside stone that has fallen over to left.*
C: *On shelter wall high above canyon floor.*
C, D: *Photos by Marita Vickroy*
A, C: *Enhanced on rock.*

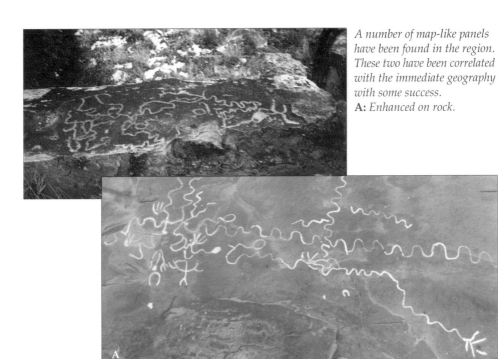

A number of map-like panels have been found in the region. These two have been correlated with the immediate geography with some success.
A: *Enhanced on rock.*

Large collection of phi-like signs. It is the most common sign found in the region, and the authors believe it may be associated with hunting. Enhanced on rock.

Pecked Abstract style petroglyphs from the foothills of the Rocky Mountains. Photo by Charles Clifton.

Petroglyph today located 15 feet above ground because of erosion of the canyon floor. Enhanced on rock.

Compass-like glyph that appears to point toward the summer solstice sunrise. Enhanced on rock. Photo by Jim Whittall.

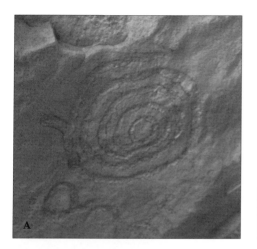

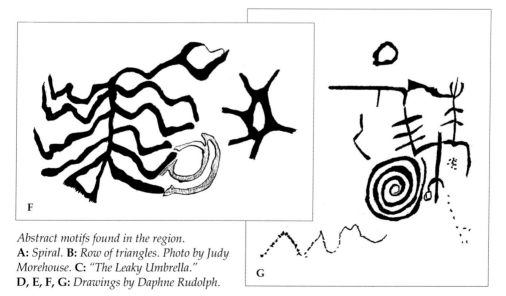

Abstract motifs found in the region.
A: *Spiral.* **B:** *Row of triangles. Photo by Judy Morehouse.* **C:** *"The Leaky Umbrella."*
D, E, F, G: *Drawings by Daphne Rudolph.*

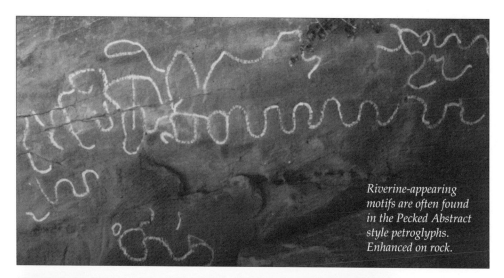

Riverine-appearing motifs are often found in the Pecked Abstract style petroglyphs. Enhanced on rock.

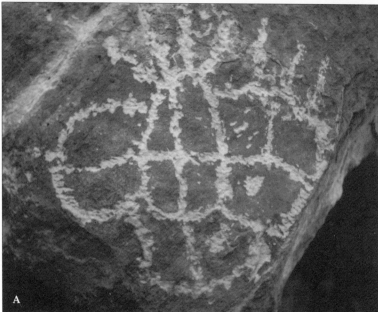

"Pretzel" motifs.
A: *Photo by Daphne Rudolph.*

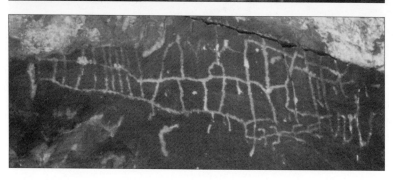

Grid-like motifs. Enhanced on rock.

Example of pecking used in making petroglyphs.

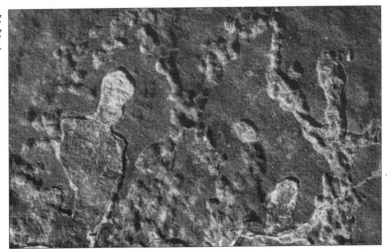

Natural formation in rock called "petromanteia" by some researchers. It resembles the Pecked Abstract style, and they claim ancient peoples tried to read such formations as messages from the gods.

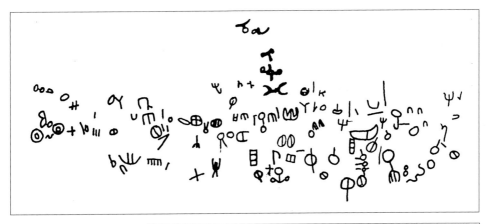

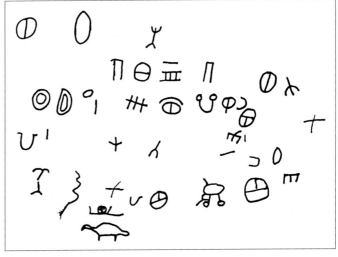

Groups of signs from Colorado that closely parallel North Arabian script together with three examples of the script from Arabia **A, B, C.** The North Arabian script was used in the Old World about the time of Christ from a few hundred years B.C. to a few hundred years A.D. A little over two dozen of the Colorado symbols are repeated from site-to-site. They are not North Arabian writing directly transferred to Colorado, since scholars are unable to read them in the same way they are read in the Old World. Research regarding other explanations is underway. Drawings are sketched on-site. All photos have glyphs enhanced on rock. Arabian inscriptions A, B, C are from Winnett and Harding (1978).

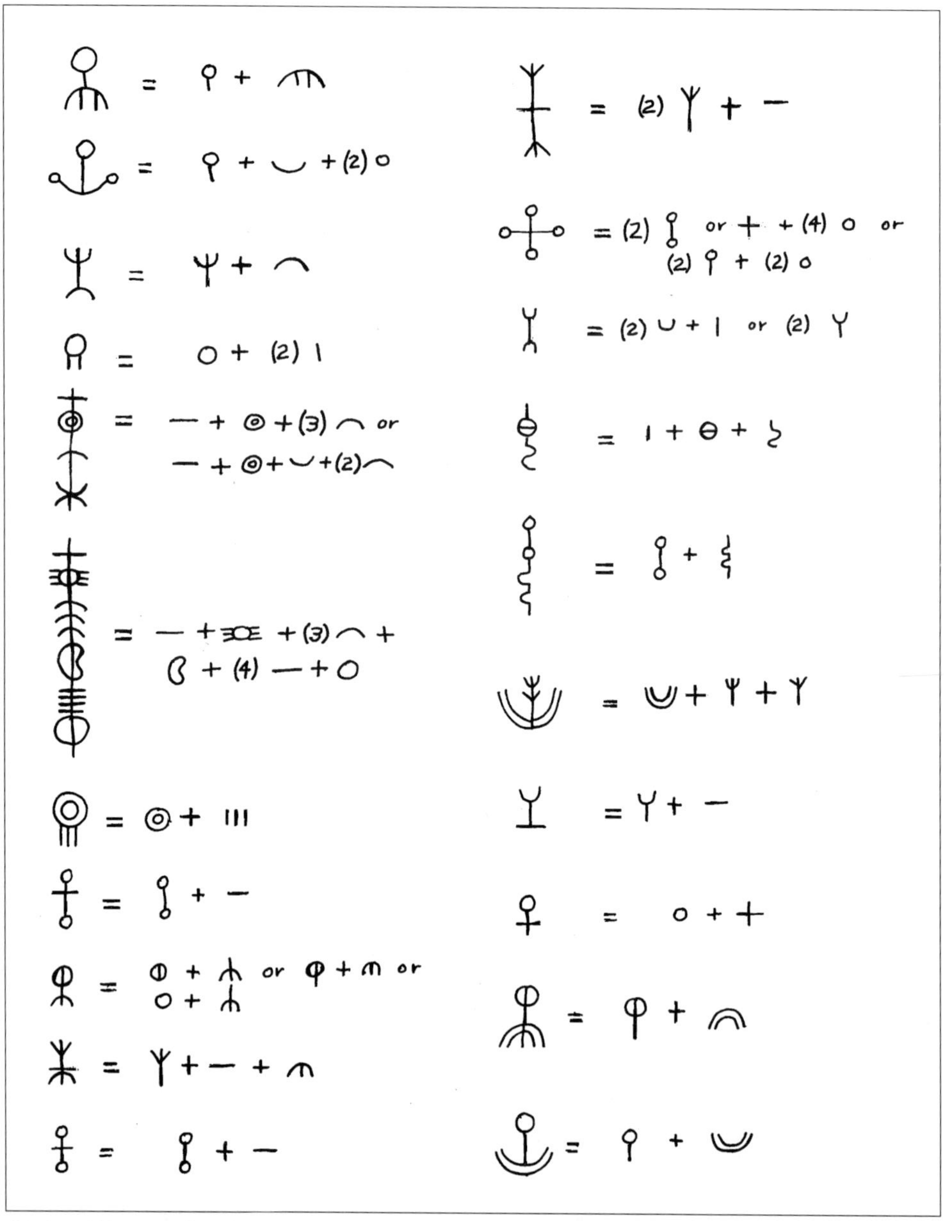

Regional ligatures (combinations) of some of the southeast Colorado signs that are similar to North Arabian script as illustrated on the previous pages. We call them ligatures because they can be broken into the commonly occurring signs as shown here. Somewhat similar combining of signs is used in Arabia for clan symbols and camel brands.

A

Combination panels, **Plate I.** *These panels contain many of the elements of the Pecked Abstract style together, such as grids, riverine-looking motifs, meanders, ligatures, "pretzels," and letter-like signs.* **A:** *Large panel with detail sections shown on pages 22 and 48.*

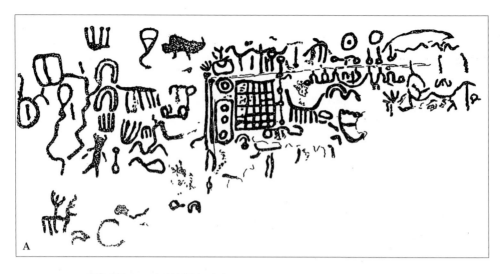

Combination panels,
Plate II. *All photos have petroglyphs enhanced on rocks.*
A: *Drawing by Jim Whittall.*

Combination panels, **Plate III.**
All photos have petroglyphs enhanced on rocks.
A: *Photo by Jim Whittall.*

Combination panel with crack in the rock face formed after petroglyphs were pecked.

Examples of large, stylized, letter-like signs.

Examples of ligatures, many of which involve rounded "pitch fork" signs.

CHAPTER 4

PECKED PICTORIAL

Petroglyphs of the Pecked Pictorial group of styles, like those in the preceding chapter, are made by pecking, but they are representational, not abstract. They almost always depict people and animals with bodies that are fully pecked out and heavily repatinated. Deer with large antlers similar to the deer petroglyphs of northeastern New Mexico are common in the southwestern portion of the region and seem to be somewhat more recent than the other Pecked Pictorial glyphs. Researchers have suggested that some of the Pecked Pictorial petroglyphs are related to the New Mexico Rio Grande style.

Many other variations of this group of styles suggest a series of sub-styles, but there is a need for further research on this subject across the whole region to establish reliable classifications. When this is done, it may be possible to associate specific styles with certain cultures, such as that of the Apishipa Focus people. The Pecked Pictorial petroglyphs seem to be primarily artistic renderings of models seen in real life by the artists, but other interpretations are possible.

Some pecked animals are found along with the abstract glyphs discussed in the previous chapter, but most occur alone or in panels of Pecked Pictorial glyphs. In several cases, due to erosion of canyon floors, the oldest glyphs are at the top, and the youngest at the bottom where more recent erosion has taken place. This is reversed from the order found in archaeological strata. Conforming to the chronology discussed in Chapter 2, the Pecked Pictorial glyphs occupy areas on such panels between the Pecked Abstract and Plains Biographic elements. At one very interesting site where a rock slide has taken place in front of an older panel, silt has filled in between the rocks covering the panel, and the more recent petroglyphs are carved above.

In the Pecked Pictorial glyphs, the pecking in many cases is very fine and quite carefully done, and the presence of zoomorphic figures suggests that certain game animals were important to the people who pecked the glyphs.

Unlike the abstract petroglyphs of the previous chapter, the Pecked Pictorial glyphs seem to be representations of items familiar even today, but they may have had deeper significance to those who made them than just artistic expression. Such significance has proved so elusive to researchers that the interpretation of petroglyphs has been a subject of considerable controversy. Attempts have been made to explain the meaning of petroglyphs as art; picture writing; doodles; a fairly universal language based on sign language; metaphoric expressions (in which a mountain lion, for example, might represent bravery or power instead of merely being the image of the animal); the mental images seen by a young brave during his vision quest; the product of shamanistic trances; alphabetic writing; and a number of others.

Conventional scholarship has traditionally embraced the interpretation of American petroglyphs as art, but has opposed the idea that they are any kind of communication system based on a form of writing because that idea has not been adequately demonstrated. Meaning is conventionally seen as locked in the mind of the original artist; however, recently there has been a move toward explanations such as vision quest or shamanistic images, especially for more distorted or highly stylized portrayals. The overview nature of this book does not permit a more detailed treatment of the interpretation question, but the authors have discussed aspects of it more fully in their previous books.

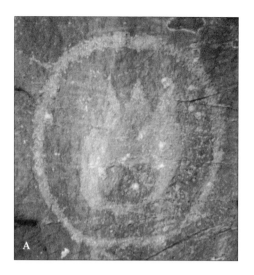

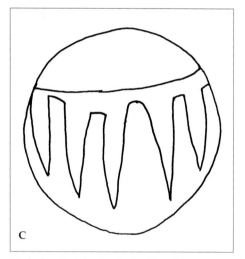
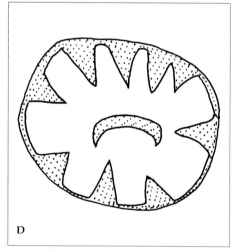

Pecked Pictorial petroglyphs thought to represent shields. **A:** *Photo by Judy Morehouse.*
B: *Enhanced on rock.* **C, D:** *Drawings traced from photos.*

Hunting scene.
Drawing by Daphne Rudolph.

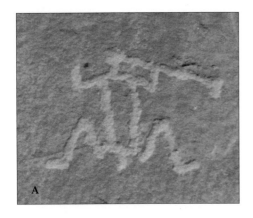

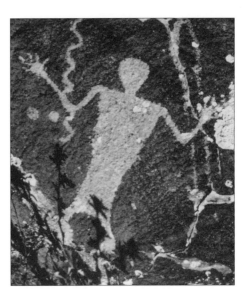

Human figure petroglyphs from the region.
A, B: *Two figures who may be flute-playing, pipe-smoking, or cloud-blowing.*
C: *Drawing traced from photo.*

A

B

C

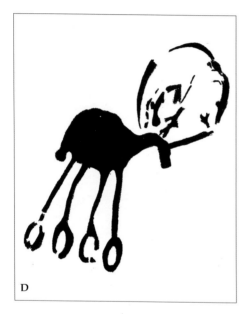

D

E

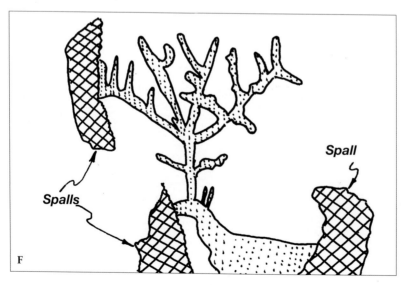

F

Spalls

Spall

Details of Pecked Pictorial antlered quadrupeds from the region.
A, B, C, D: *Drawings by Daphne Rudolph.*
E, F: *Drawings traced from photos.*
G: *Photo by Marita Vickroy.*
H: *Photo by Daphne Rudolph.*
I: *Enhanced on rock.*

A: *Panel of animals with very unusual antlers.*
B: *Detail of multi-tined antlers that may represent a non-typical Mule Deer. Somewhat similar antlers do occur in nature. Photos by Judy Morehouse.*

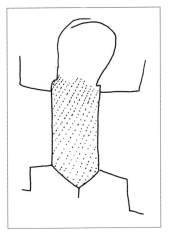

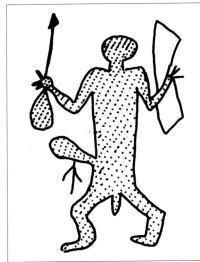

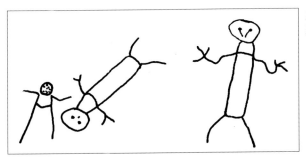

Pecked Pictorial petroglyphs of human figures traced from photos.

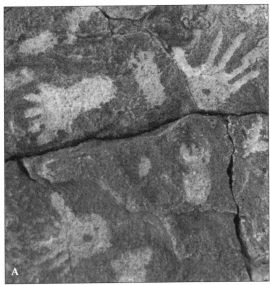

Many hand and foot petroglyphs, some with extra digits, are found around the region.
A: *Photo by Marita Vickroy.*

Panels of animals in conjunction with phi-like signs. Animals are frequently shown with these symbols protruding from their bodies, possibly representing fletched missiles, such as arrows.
A: *Photo by Marita Vickroy.*
B: *Enhanced on photo.*
C: *Enhanced on rock.*

*Animals conventionally interpreted as sheep.
Photos by Marita Vickroy.*

*Interesting variation with
horns on backwards.*

Petroglyph of dog-like animal on boulder.

Animal with trail of tracks. Enhanced on rock.

Panels from the region showing large groups of antlered quadrupeds.
A: *Photo by Daphne Rudolph.*
B, F, G: *Drawings by Daphne Rudolph.*
C, D: *Enhanced on rock.*
E: *From Loendorf and Kuehn (1991).*

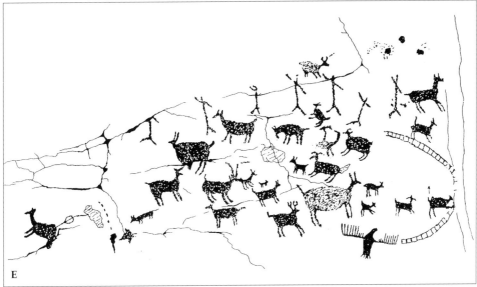

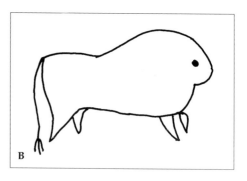

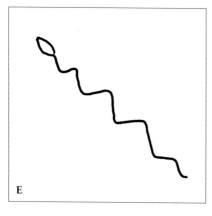

Other Pecked Pictorial animal life from the region.
A, G: *Enhanced on rock.*
B, E: *Drawings traced from photos.*
C, D: *Drawings by Daphne Rudolph.*
F: *Photo by Marita Vickroy.*
G: *"The Quail Hunt."*
H: *Photo by Alma Barker.*
I: *Photo by Judy Morehouse.*

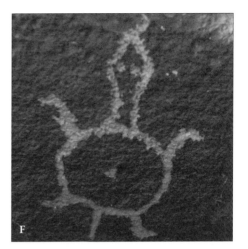

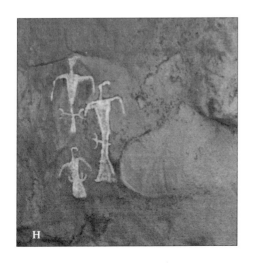

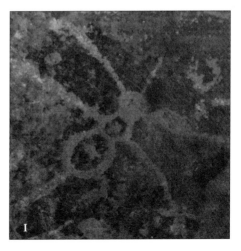

CHAPTER 5

PLAINS BIOGRAPHIC

The Plains Biographic style petroglyphs are thought to have been made by the various Plains Indians who have occupied the region in the last 500 years or so. No attempt will be made here to sort the petroglyphs out by specific tribe of origin or substyle. Generally, they are relatively unpatinated figures of animals or people. They are most often incised or engraved in outline by abrading rather than by pecking as in the previously mentioned styles. They are not as numerous or widespread as the Pecked Abstract but appear more concentrated at sites where people may have lived; some occur singly and some in groups at what may have been ritual sites. In a few cases, a figure is both abraded and painted; however, this is rare, and the painting may have been added later. In other cases, later glyphs may be superimposed on those of a previous style.

Often, later petroglyphs are carved over earlier ones. Here, a Plains Biographic horse is superimposed on glyphs of the Pecked Abstract style.

The authors have attempted to reproduce petroglyphs experimentally that are similar in appearance to those found in southeast Colorado, but as explained in Chapter 3, we have been unsuccessful in producing similar pecked glyphs by impact with hammerstones or other tools. On the other hand, we have discovered that abraded grooves can easily be made in unvarnished sandstone, but they are very difficult to produce on heavily patinated surfaces. Stone axes, arrowheads, bone tools, antlers, sticks, or even fingernails can be successfully employed in abrading, especially if the stone is unpatinated and relatively soft or wet. By studying the shape, depth, and cross section of grooves, it is possible to learn something of the tool that made them. Other techniques used in the region such as boring, rubbing, and incising have been easily reproduced by us, using a variety of tools. All experiments were made on talus stones at the authors' homes.

Modeling clay impressions of grooves that had been made in sandstone by the authors with various instruments. The cross sections of the grooves suggest what was used to make them. From left to right the tools used were: blade edge of a stone axe; deer antler; shaped rock; arrowhead.

Many of the Plains Biographic petroglyphs are rather crudely executed, but some are quite artistic. Some stylistic elements repeat from site to site: thunderbirds, horses like those in the Plains Indians' winter counts, snakes, deer, and buffalo, for example. Panels that may depict historical events are said to be present. Carol Patterson-Rudolph has interpreted one such panel as the Indians' version of a battle with the U. S. Cavalry.

Surprisingly, one petroglyph seems to picture a humpbacked flute-player like Kokopelli, a common figure in Southwestern rock art. Two other Pecked Pictorial figures (page 36) resemble the related "cloud blowers" of the Pueblo Indians. No secure correspondences have yet been established to the Anasazi petroglyphs of southwest Colorado, but many of the engravings of people are stylistically similar to those in the plains of Wyoming, Montana, and Alberta; and tepee rings are found near some of the Plains Biographic sites. As with the other styles of the region, Plains Biographic petroglyphs occur where people would have lived, hunted, and farmed—along the streams and in the canyons.

A

B

On September 8, 1868, a band of Cheyenne Dog Soldiers raided Boggsville, the first non-fortified settlement in southeast Colorado. They killed one settler and stole several horses. The cavalry from Ft. Lyon pursued the Cheyennes in a running battle for over 40 miles, finally pinning down some of them in a rocky ravine. Four Indians and two soldiers were killed and one soldier was wounded in the ensuing firefight. The site became known as Bloody Spring and a petroglyph (**A**) carved on the ceiling of the grotto there records the chase and fight according to Carol Patterson-Rudolph. She wrote, "putting the story together, the symbols suggest to me a long chase with stolen horses" (Patterson 1985). **B:** The entire affair was re-enacted at Boggsville by regional residents in September of 1993, at the time of the Santa Fe Trail Symposium in La Junta. **A:** From Patterson (1985).

Human figures in Plains Biographic style, **Plate I. A:** *Humpbacked flute-player reminiscent of Kokopelli.* **B:** *Figures withtear streaks similar to those more common farther west, in Utah.* **C:** *Painted after engraving.* **D, E, F:** *Enhanced on rock.*

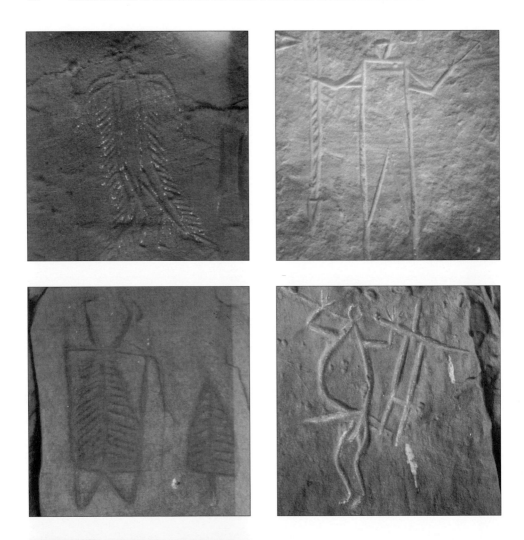

Human figures in Plains Biographic Style,
Plate II.

Human figures in Plains Biographic Style,
Plate III.

Plains Biographic human figures traced from photographs, **Plate I.**

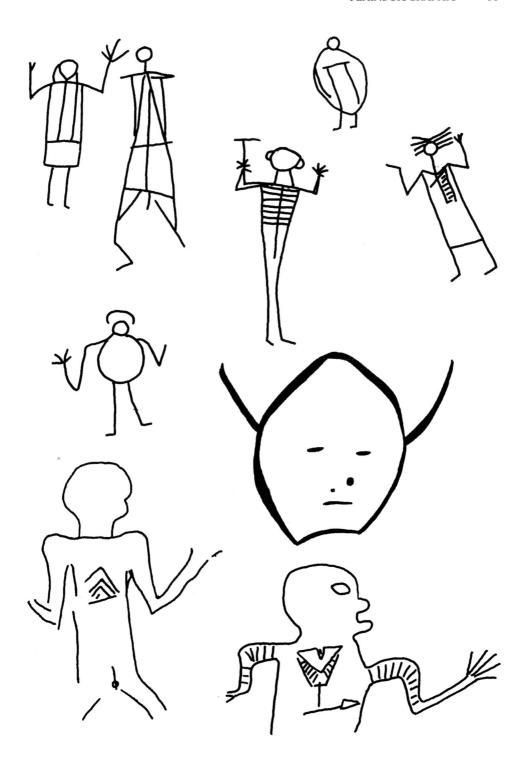

Plains Biographic human figures traced from photographs, **Plate II.**

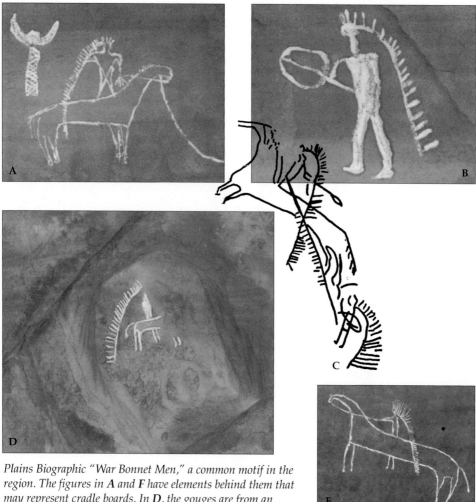

*Plains Biographic "War Bonnet Men," a common motif in the region. The figures in **A** and **F** have elements behind them that may represent cradle boards. In **D**, the gouges are from an attempt by someone to remove the petroglyph from the bedrock. **F**: Enhanced on the photo. **A, B, D, E**: Enhanced on rock. **C**: Drawing traced from photo.*

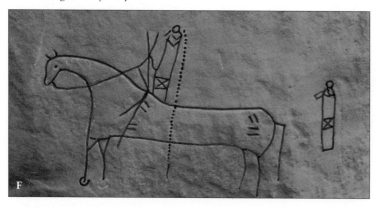

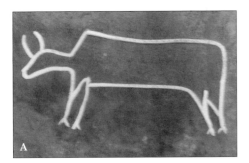
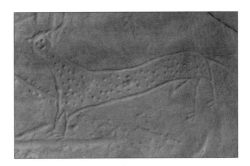

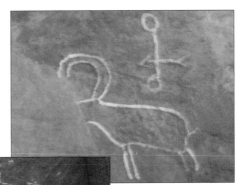

Animals in Plains Biographic style.
A: *Photo by Alma Barker.*
B: *Painted after engraving.*
C: *Photo by Marita Vickroy.*

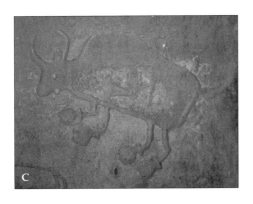

Plains Biographic petroglyphs traced from photos. **Plate I.**

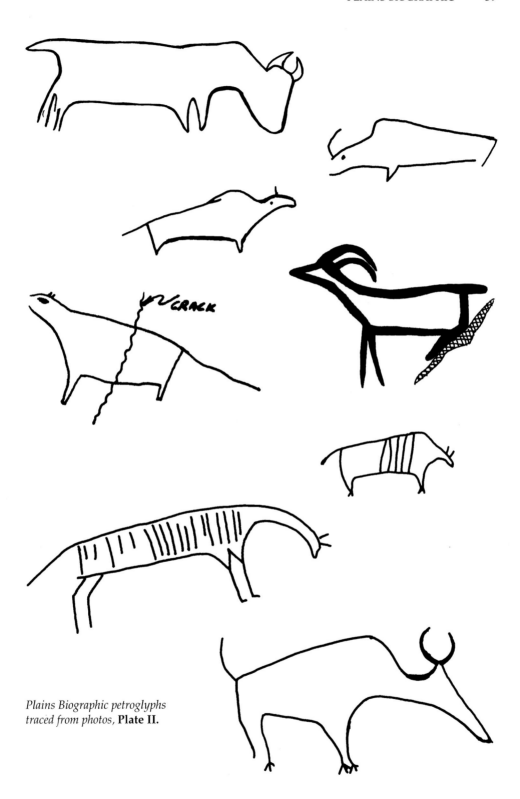

CRACK

Plains Biographic petroglyphs
traced from photos, **Plate II.**

Plains Biographic bird petroglyphs,
Plate I.
A: *Enhanced on rock. Photo by Marita Vickroy.*

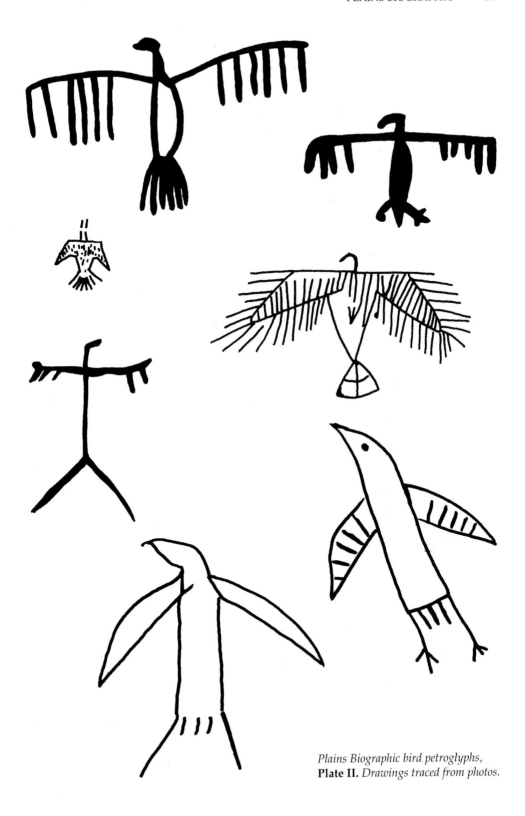

Plains Biographic bird petroglyphs,
Plate II. *Drawings traced from photos.*

Copulating couple motif found at three sites within a 60-mile range.

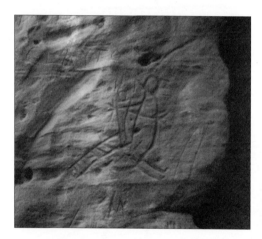

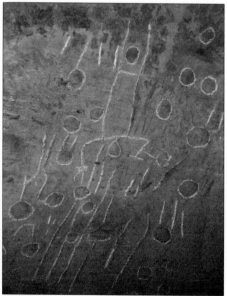

"The Wedding." Enhanced on rock. Photo by Alma Barker.

"Indian Baby Rock," said locally to be either a site where Indian women went to give birth and gouged out cupules or where young couples came and let blood to become fertile. Enhanced on rock.

"The Battle Scene."
Drawing by Jim Whittall.

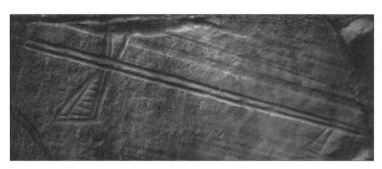

Glyph interpreted as either a tomahawk, peace pipe, or combination of them.

Details of large Plains Biographic panel shown on book covers.

Panel with plumed-serpent-like head in center.

"Tree of Life"

"Man With Hat" scene depicting human figures, bear, buffalo, and "target."

CHAPTER 6

PARALLEL LINES

Rows of straight parallel lines from various time periods are found throughout the world. They have been suggested to be counts or tallies, calendars, decoration, tool-working marks, doodles, and even writing. Southeast Colorado has many such markings, perhaps intended for several of these purposes. A number of the groups of lines seem purposefully composed, suggesting they may have had special significance for the engravers.

Some of these marks may be Ogam writing, a possibility the authors have been investigating. Ogam is an alphabet that was used in the British Isles in the first half of the first millennium A.D. primarily to mark gravestones. As used there a stemline is either drawn or implied, and letters are represented by marks in groups of one to five above, below, or across the stemline. Vowels are shown by short tick-marks on the stemline, which is usually the vertical corner of a stone.

We believe it is probable that a somewhat earlier version of Ogam, dated possibly as early as 1000 B.C., is found in a limited portion of southeast Colorado. This Ogam has no vowels and is usually written horizontally on a flat surface with the stemline drawn. Proposed readings of some of the inscriptions identify certain solar alignments that interact with the glyphs, as described in Chapter 9 of this book. Few scholars accept the Ogam identification or the implication of pre-Columbian Old World visitation suggested by this interpretation. The debate over this issue is covered more fully in our previous books (McGlone and Leonard 1986, McGlone et al. 1993).

Most of the straight parallel markings other than the possible Ogamic material are much more recent (<500 years old) and must have some explanation other than Ogam. Often they are dismissed as "axe-sharpening" marks, but sharpening the edge of a stone axe does not leave a groove with the canoe-like shape of these markings. An axe would only be dulled if rubbed in a manner that would produce such a groove. Yet some of the markings may be tool *working* marks of some type. Rubbing bone tools to point them can leave such markings, and polishing out the peck marks left in an axe from shaping it can also leave such grooves, although as a group they should show the varying widths and cross sections of the contours of the axe. Grooves made by stone tools can account for some of the more random groups of vertical lines, but this explanation seems unlikely for the large rows of even, well-organized markings. These are more likely to have been made for some purpose other than tool working—counts or tallies, perhaps.

One other style of straight-parallel-line groupings from the region is the type we have given the code name "Music", although we do not intend to imply that they actually are a form of music. Actually these Music glyphs are parallel, pecked lines hanging from a long horizontal line, and the fact that they sometimes end in pecked-out circles suggested musical notes to us. One of the Music glyphs is 69 feet long and has been dated to some 1800 years ago. Thus, it falls into the overlapping period of the Pecked Abstract and Pecked Pictorial styles.

Because they are so simple in form and not pictorial, the potential significance of the different types of glyphs composed of parallel lines is easily overlooked; but they may have had their own special purposes, and should be studied with this possibility in mind.

Ogam alphabet. **A:** *As used in the British Isles.* **B:** *As used in the southeast Colorado region.*

Ogam-like markings from the region. **A, B:** *Colorado inscription showing Ogamic stroke placement and grouping.* **C, D:** *Two regional inscriptions for which Ogam readings have been proposed. See McGlone et al. (1993) for details. Conventional scholars have neither accepted the Ogam interpretation nor offered reasonable alternative explanations.*

Group of horizontal parallel lines with apparent age of the Plains Biographic style. The lines have common terminations in groups of 9 and 18.

Tool-sharpening marks produced by sharpening the cutting edge of a stone axe, one side at a time.

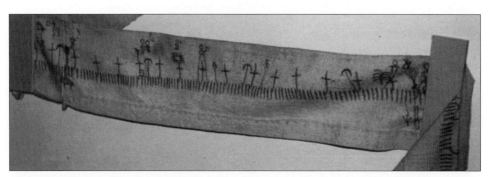

Kiowa calendar (ca 1920) from Panhandle Plains Museum, Canyon, Texas, that some have suggested may explain some of the parallel marks of the region.

Groups of parallel lines not reasonably interpretable as Ogam writing.

Unusual straight line markings from the Plains Biographic period.

Ogam-like marks on a stone found on top of a rock cairn.

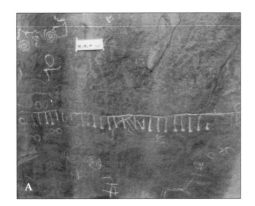

Parallel-line petro-glyphs we have given the code name "Music," because of their note-like appearance as in A and B.
C: *Section of 69-foot-long Music glyph. Enhanced on rock.* **D:** *Ted Barker standing beside upside-down Music glyphs on boulder that toppled over when undermined by flow of river. Enhanced on rock. Photo by Judy Morehouse.*

CHAPTER 7

COWBOYS AND SETTLERS

The presence of people of European ancestry in southeast Colorado is shown by the graffiti of Spaniards, Mexicans, Euroamericans, and possibly Basques, all constituting the Historic European style in the table on page 16, made since the time of Columbus. Coronado may have moved through this region in the 1540s, and two sets of petroglyphs are claimed to have been carved by his expedition. The Purgatoire River got its name from Spanish soldiers who supposedly died there without absolution by a priest, and several early Spanish artifacts have been found in its tributaries. Rock walls, intended sometimes as fences, sometimes as corrals, and possibly sometimes merely as territorial markers are also present. Some were probably built by early sheepherders and others by later cattlemen.

Bent's Old Fort near present day La Junta on the Arkansas River was a focal point for the fur trade and for the American presence in the first half of the nineteenth century. The famous scout Kit Carson lived in Boggsville near the town of Las Animas. Bent's Fort has been restored as a National Historic Site, and Boggsville is under restoration today. The sites of at least two U. S. Cavalry actions with the Indians are known, and stories are told of outlaws' hideouts and their confrontations with pursuing posses. The original Mountain Branch of the Santa Fe Trail as well as the later Cimarron Cutoff and the Granada-Ft.Union Wagon Road went through the area, but the principal use of the land today is for cattle ranching.

These activities have generated the many interesting graffiti that are scattered about the region. Names, often with dates, are the most common; and it almost seems that everyone wanted to register his presence. We have followed the perambulations of one cowboy, B. Kelley, over much of the region by finding his name in 25 places. Travelers on the Santa Fe Trail left their names along it. Some are elaborately engraved, but most carvers seem to have been satisfied just to note their passing. Kit Carson's signature has been found in four places. In many places in the West, Basque people have left distinctive carvings on rocks and trees; however, to date we have not found any graffiti in the region that are demonstrably Basque.

More artistic graffiti exist as well, varying from cowboy cartoons to religious symbols. A few are even sculpted in relief. The European graffiti are distributed much like the Plains Biographic glyphs and occur at many of the same sites, but they too are not as widely distributed as the Pecked Abstract.

One particularly interesting example is what may be the grave marker for an Arab camel driver. Before the Civil War, the U.S. Army experimented with the use of camels in the dry portions of the West, assisted by Arab camel drivers. The Disney movie "Hawmps" tells this story in a comedic version. The Arab leader was called "Hi-Jolly", for Haj Ali, and he is buried in Quartzite, Arizona, under a pyramid-shaped tombstone. The Army released its camels into the wild when the Civil War broke out, but camels were tried many years later in commercial enterprises. As a young boy, Ted Barker was told of such a caravan by a man who had seen the camels in southeastern Colorado in the early 1900s. Near that spot, today, there is a pyramid-shaped stone with an Arab name, the date 1902, the drawing of a camel, and the word "CAML" on it.

The widespread presence of the European graffiti shows the equally widespread presence of people in historic times. Interestingly, the canyons are much less populated today than they were nearly a century ago. Smaller ranches and homesteads have coalesced into the much larger ranches of today, significantly reducing the population density.

Petroglyphs purportedly left along the Cimarron River by the Coronado entrada on its return from Kansas. **A:** *Signature, "Coronatto 1541," attributed to two Italian adventurers on the expedition. Photo by Pam Valdez.* **B:** *"Compass" on floor of cave a few miles from the signature inscription. Some Coronado researchers claim both to be authentic (Etter 1984), although this is dubious in the view of most scholars, who believe that Coronado probably did not travel this far north.*

Military signatures from the region. **A:** *Traced from photo.* **B:** *Photo by Timothy Aschauer.*

Civilian signatures from stops along the Santa Fe Trail. One man, Jesus M. Pacheco signed twice in 1862.

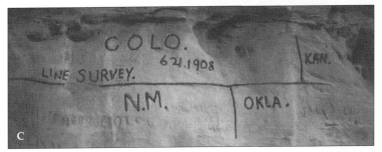

Other interesting civilian signatures. **A:** *One of four possible Kit Carson signatures in the region. The authors consider this one probably authentic because of verbal history within Carson's family, who still own the ranch where it is carved. Photo by Ruth Smith.* **B:** *Sebaranio Romero carved his name over Indian pictographs.* **C:** *Glyph left by state-line survey crew.* **D:** *J.A. Cardoba reversed the 9 in 1890.* **E:** *Enhanced on photograph.*

"Cowboy cartoons" from the region.

A group of crosses of various types. The third cross is shown below and on page 76.

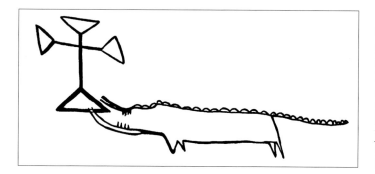

One of the above cross types, apparently being eaten by an alligator. The authors would appreciate input on the possible significance of this glyph and the above four crosses that are carved nearby. Drawing traced from photo.

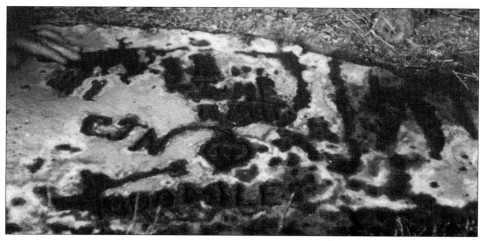

The last day of an outlaw. Inscription in a rock shelter near a spring, where a wounded fugitive from justice was trapped and killed by a pursuing posse. Apparently he was homesick and inscribed a heart, the date, his initials, and "1000 miles" on the rock, indicating that his heart was 1000 miles from home. The father of Ken Curtis, who played Festus on Gunsmoke, *is reputed to have been a member of the posse.*

Brands from the region. **A:** *Triangle-L, shown as used.* **B:** *Bar-M plus the name Karen.* **C:** *Brand VIC converted to steer's head.*

These inscriptions refer to Butte City, Colorado, a small settlement about 1 1/2 miles northwest of Two Buttes Peak. Everything there burned and the people moved to the nearby present town of Two Buttes, chartered in 1909.

Record of a wide-ranging cowboy, Benjamin Kelley, who worked cattle at many locations across the region. We have found the signature, "B. Kelley," at 25 places, sometimes with the B backwards.
A: *Kelley was a member of the Odd Fellows Lodge, number 11, of Las Animas, Colorado, and often drew symbols of the lodge near his name.* **B:** *Old Odd Fellows Lodge building with Kelley signature. Enhanced on rock.*

This glyph of a soldier is located in a rock shelter behind a defensive rock wall, apparently built by the cavalry during a winter campaign against the Indians. The arrow through the head is made with a larger-pointed tool than the rest of the glyph and could have been added later. The man also has a "weeping eye," possibly indicating he had been wounded. Drawing traced from photo.

"Chinese" character found on boulder. Drawing traced from photo.

Record left by camel expedition. See text for details.

"The Conquistador." Photo by Marita Vickroy. Enhanced on photo.

Bas relief engraving of a dove. Photo by Susan Touchstone.

Recent menorah petroglyph as originally carved. The menorah has since been used by a restorer to test tinted fillers in a range of shades and perhaps a variety of materials. Portions of the grooves have been filled with the test materials.

"The Priest." Photo by Susan Touchstone.

Detail from large petroglyph panel on book covers.

Steer petroglyph near spring in the Comanche Grasslands. Drawing traced from photo.

Three dimensional-appearing glyph.

*Recent abstract petroglyph elements. **A:** Figure known variously as the Eternal Knot, Filfot Cross, Solomon's Cross, and the Interlocking Cross. This motif is sacred to some of the southeastern Indians and also occurs in a large geoglyph along the Colorado River. **B:** Swastika variant.*

CHAPTER 8

ASSORTED PICTOGRAPHS

Pictographs are paintings applied to rock surfaces much as an artist might paint a canvas, although fingers may have sometimes been used instead of brushes made of plant fibers or fur. Pictographs are not nearly as common in southeast Colorado as petroglyphs, and are executed in numerous styles and colors, including red, yellow, blue, and black. Paint was made by grinding pigments such as ochre (red or yellow), into organic binding agents like blood, fat, or eggs. The organic nature of these vehicles makes it possible to obtain radiocarbon dates for pictographs today, although to our knowledge no such testing has been carried out in the region covered by this book.

A few of the southeast Colorado pictographs appear to share motifs with the Pecked Abstract petroglyph style. Many are similar to the Plains Biographic style, which contains images of horses. No attempt will be made to suggest age, style, or the people who made the pictographs until more research has been performed by specialists. One particularly interesting style, present at two sites, has elongated stick men with short bowed legs painted in red. The men are carrying what appear to be weapons that resemble double-weighted atlatls (spear throwers). No similar figures have been found in the petroglyphs. Also present are animals struck by arrows. The pictographs at both sites look relatively fresh but are located in rock shelters where recently washed away silt could have protected them for an unknown period.

Researchers formerly believed that pictographs would not last very long when exposed to the elements and thus must be relatively recent. Current research shows that pigments actually seep into rock surfaces, staining them and making it possible for existing pictographic images to be very old. Some of the paintings show great care and artistic skill in their preparation and seemingly demonstrate the interest of the creators in their environment.

Not only did early artists use rock walls of the region for their canvases, but so did recent residents. An excellent example is found along the upper reaches of the Purgatoire River in a side canyon that is a modern day art gallery. An artist, Martin Bowden, lived there and painted the canyon walls with numerous images of animals and historic Americans. An eagle is painted high on a cliff face, and a larger-than-life rattlesnake is painted coiled on a rock beside the trail. Although these may not be pictographs in the usual historical sense, we include them, because future generations will undoubtedly consider them to be such.

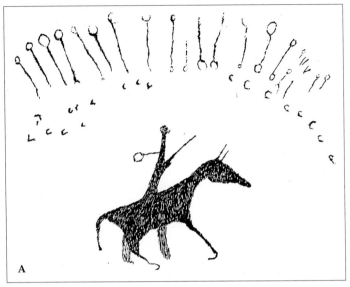

A

B

Three painted panels from the Purgatoire River shown in Loendorf and Kuehn (1991). **A:** *They interpret the figure, painted in red and black, as a rider who has doubled back (U-shaped tracks) and has been fired on by gunshots (tailed circles) and hit.* **B:** *They interpret the black figure as an owl painted by a Euroamerican artist.* **C:** *They interpret this black or dark gray panel as a travois and two horses.*

C

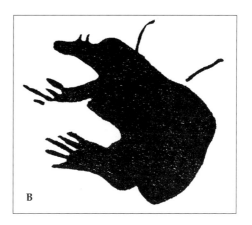

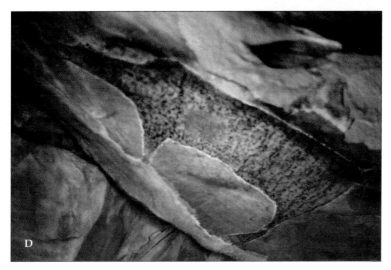

Bear images are common in the region. **A:** *Drawing by Daphne Rudolph.* **B:** *From Loendorf and Kuehn (1991).* **C:** *Bear reported locally in the 1870s and nationally in the 1880s. Michelle McFarlane in front of bear.* **D:** *Painted in black except red spot behind front leg. Photo by Don Vickroy.*

Badly faded, reddish-brown human figures and two birds that may represent an Indian myth of the shamanistic transformation of a man to a bird-like figure. Figures enhanced on the photo.

Details from a row of about two dozen muskets or rifles, painted in red. Figures enhanced on the photo.

Geometric, red-painted signs from the back of a rock shelter.

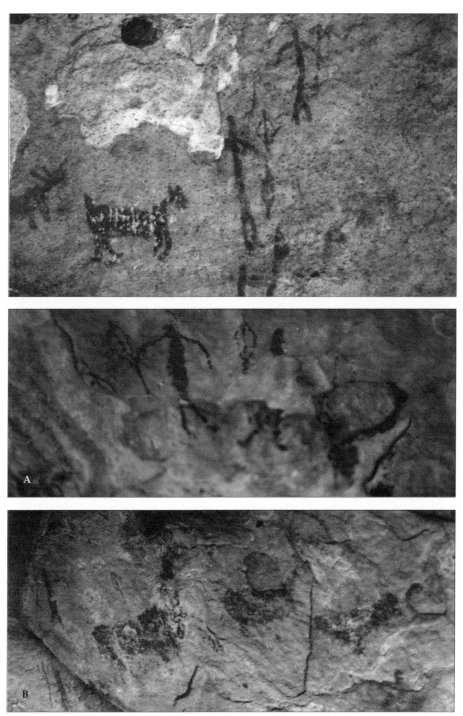

Hunting scenes painted in red. The men seem to be carrying some kind of spear thrower (atlatl); and arrows (darts) are shown near animals or in their backs. **A:** *Photo by Marita Vickroy.* **B:** *Photo by Greg Westfall.*

Unusual red-painted elements from ceiling of large rockshelter 12 feet off floor. The authors are interested in hearing possible interpretations of the paintings from readers.

Men on horseback. **A:** *Red painted, shield-bearing Indians.* **B:** *Unknown rider, painted in red.*

Animals painted in red. **A:** *Wild pig or bear.* **B:** *Buffalo.* **C:** *Unknown animal and linear markings.*

Modern art gallery in a side canyon of the Purgatoire River. Martin Bowden retired to a lonesome life in the canyon in 1911 and lived there until his self-inflicted death in 1958. Known as the "Hermit of the Purgatoire" or "Picasso of the Purgatoire," he painted about 40 life-size figures of animals and people on the sandstone walls with brightly colored house-paint. **A:** Photo by Karl Wheeler. **B:** Photo by Margaret Goodrich.

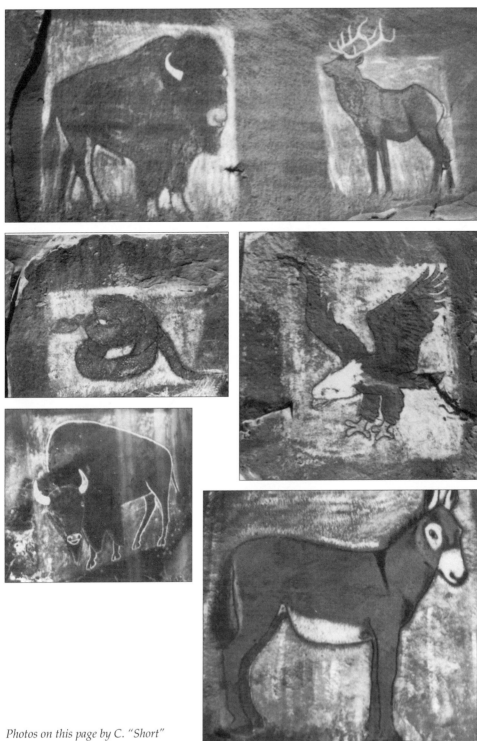

Photos on this page by C. "Short" Watters.

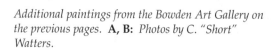

Additional paintings from the Bowden Art Gallery on the previous pages. **A, B:** *Photos by C. "Short" Watters.*

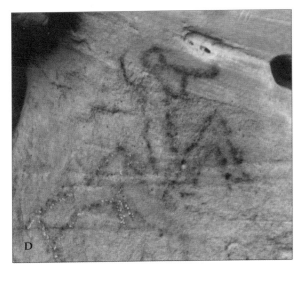

*Human figures. **A:** Red-painted group of people. **B:** Man with unusual headdress painted in blue. Drawing traced from photo. **C:** Warrior painted in blue. **D:** Man in blue playing flute, smoking, or cloud blowing.*

CHAPTER 9

ARCHAEOASTRONOMY

Archaeoastronomy is a relatively new discipline that studies the ancients' use of astronomy in their religion and everyday life. Many early people were sun worshippers and others used the point of the rising or setting sun on the horizon to regulate their calendars—to know when to plant crops or begin ceremonies for example. The farthest north and south of these horizon positions occur on the summer and winter solstices, the longest and shortest days of the year. The equinoxes, occurring twice a year in March and September, are the days when the sun rises and sets due east and west, halfway between the solstice points on the horizon, and are days of equal day and night.

Ancient people may have marked these special days, and others, by constructing alignments with the sun that often involved petroglyphs. Some may be direct viewing sites, where an observer could have placed his head at a petroglyph to view the sun. The site is set up so that the rising or setting sun is seen in a notch in the horizon or over a wooden post or stone. Other alignments may be indirect and may have operated with shadows or beams of light falling on petroglyphic targets. Southeast Colorado has some outstanding archaeoastronomical sites of both the direct and indirect types.

A spectacular Colorado site is Crack Cave, where the rising equinox sun lights a group of straight lines we interpret as Ogam writing. The glyph is some 15 feet into a cave formed by a large crack in the cliff face. This site is in Picture Canyon on the Comanche National Grasslands where it is protected by the U.S. Forest Service. A video of the alignment operating on the equinox is available for viewing, through the Baca County Historical Society in Springfield, Colorado. The town now has a biannual Equinox Festival based on the Crack Cave alignment.

Another important site, called the Anubis Caves, is in the Oklahoma Panhandle. It has two panels with solar alignments that operate on the equinoxes. In one, a face-shaped shadow falls on a ruler-like inscription, and advances one mark on the ruler each day for the 12 days before the equinox in September and after the equinox in March. The other panel has a light and shadow display involving a complex set of images, containing alignments specific to the day of the equinox. Both are described in detail in our previous books, with a suggested cosmological interpretation of the site.

All of the previously described alignments are of the indirect type with light or shadow falling on a glyph. Another Colorado site, which we call the Sun Temple, is of the direct type. When one places his head in a "sun-ring" petroglyph and looks toward the horizon, he can view the sun rising in a shoulder of the cliff, framed on three sides by the cliff and the mesa. This event occurs on the cross-quarter days in August and May, when the sun rises about midway in time between the summer solstice and the equinox. The cross-quarter days were of importance to several ancient peoples and were used, for example, to set the calendar of the ancient Celts.

These sites are quite old, dating to more than 2000 years ago based on the age of the petroglyphs, and most interestingly, all contain Ogamic markings, through whose interpretation the alignments were found. Two other sites currently under study involve alignments with the sun at the time of the winter solstice.

At least three other sites with solar alignments have been found that were made by much later people. They operate on the counted equinox instead of the true equinox as in the previous examples. The counted equinox is determined by dividing in half the number of days between the time of the solstices; the result is about two days from the time of the true equinox, and the sun rises slightly off a due east sunrise point. This is because of the varying rate of the motion of the earth around the sun throughout the year.

Later people in southeast Colorado appear to have employed the counted equinox in their solar alignments. One alignment is built into a large Apishipa Focus circle set prominently on a bench above the Purgatoire River. Two stones arranged like a rifle sight align with the rising sun about two days from the true equinox. The other two sites are indirect alignments operating on the counted equinox, with light and shadow falling on Plains Biographic petroglyphs.

Several other possible solar alignments have been identified in the region and are under study. Caution must be exercised in archaeoastronomical research because the possibility of fortuitous configurations of natural formations is ever present, and the intent of the architect of an alignment is difficult to demonstrate with certainty. We consider those described here to have a high probability of having been constructed by ancient people with the purposes explained, primarily because of the involvement and nature of the petroglyphs.

Archaeoastronomy of the Crack Cave in Picture Canyon on the Comanche National Grasslands. Springfield, Colorado, now has a biannual Equinox Festival based on this phenomenon.
A: *Crack Cave before installation of protective cage.*
B: *Crack Cave with protective cage.*
C: *Inscription in Crack Cave whose interpretation as Ogam led to the discovery of its illumination by the equinox sunrise as shown on the next page.*

Direct-viewing solar alignment at the site called the Sun Temple, which operates on cross-quarter days as described in the text on page 97.

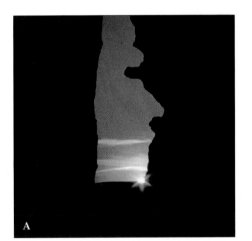
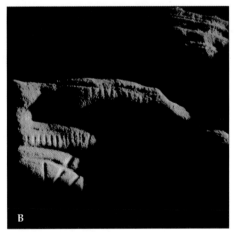

*Lighting of the Crack Cave inscription by the equinox sunrise. **A:** Sunrise from the cave.*
***B:** Lighting at sunrise on equinox with the illumination fitting the shape of the inscription.*

Petroglyph thought to represent a star constellation using plus marks as stars.

Counted-equinox sunset alignment involving a Plans Biographic petroglyph, the cave wall, and the horizon. Photo by Pam Valdez.

So-called Anubis panel, named for the interpretation by Gloria Farley of the dog-like figure at upper left center as the Egyptian jackal-god Anubis, based on the animal's appearance and the presence of a crown and flail.

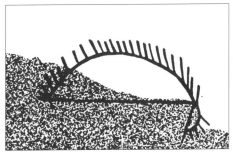
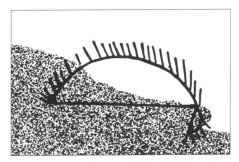

Solar alignment on the Anubis panel of page 100, is shown in lighted area. The "Thumb Pointer" comes to rest in the "Dangling Sun" petroglyph with great precision just at sunset on the equinox. See McGlone et al. (1993) for full details.
A: *One half hour before sunset.*
B: *At moment of sunset.*
C: *Drawing of alignment on equinox.*
D: *Drawing of sunset alignment one day from equinox.*

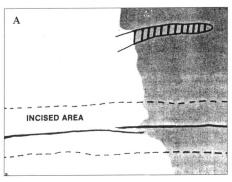
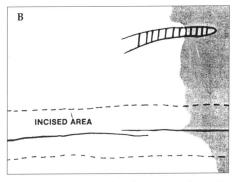

Second solar alignment at the Anubis Caves, which counts days before or after the equinox. See text.
A: *Shadow indicating one day from equinox.*
B: *Eight days from equinox. Shadow is read when the pointer shadow is on the stemline of the possible Ogam inscription in the incised area. See page 67 for photo of the Ogamic marks. Reading as Ogam suggested the equinox, an association that led to the discovery of this alignment and that above. Drawings by David Deal.*

Newly discovered, direct-type solar alignment operating on the winter solstice.
A: *Possible Ogam writing from which the sunrise can be viewed. Enhanced on rock.*
B: *Sunrise in notch formed by boulder and horizon when viewed from inscription **A**.*
C: *Double-shouldered pointer shadow associated with parallel markings at sunrise on the winter solstice.*

CHAPTER 10

PUBLIC SITES

As explained earlier, most of the sites illustrated here are on private land and are closed to viewing by the general public. One purpose of this book is to make it possible for people to see representative petroglyphs without intruding on landowners' privacy. For those who do want to see some of the actual glyphs and get a sense of the beauty and remoteness of the country, there are six sites on public land that can be visited. The U. S. Forest Service administers four of the sites, the U.S. Army Corps of Engineers the fifth, and the State of Colorado the sixth; it is located in the Apishipa State Wildlife Area.

Picture Canyon, located in the Comanche National Grasslands, some 35 miles southwest of Springfield, Colorado, near the Oklahoma state line, has examples of most of the styles described here and contains the Crack Cave solar alignment discussed in the previous chapter. There are also petroglyphs at other sites on the southern portion of the Grasslands, including one discovered as this book goes to press. Details regarding accessibility of all of these sites are available at the U. S. Forest Service office in Springfield.

Another important site, on the northern portion of the Grasslands, is Vogel Canyon, a side canyon of the Purgatoire south of La Junta, Colorado. It has excellent examples of the Pecked Abstract style and others. Access to the site is a 3/8 mile trail from a parking lot, which can be reached by driving 13 miles south of La Junta on paved Colorado 109 and following signs on a dirt road three miles to the lot.

One other petroglyph area that can be visited on U. S. Forest Service land is the Picket Wire Canyonlands. The petroglyph sites there are in a remote section of the Purgatoire River canyon accessible by a long hike or a guided four-wheel-drive auto tour. This area has not only several interesting petroglyph sites but also what is said to be the most extensive dinosaur trackway in the world. Details of visitation and accessibility restrictions are available at the U.S. Forest Service Office in La Junta.

Finally, there is a large site (5BN7) in Bent County that is open to public access. It is perhaps the single most profusely marked petroglyph site in the region and has glyphs in several styles, particularly the Pecked Abstract. The glyphs are on cliff faces and large boulders, and there are some difficulties in access because of rattlesnakes and copious quantities of poison ivy. Recently, the Colorado Archaeological Society began a major project to record the petroglyphs. The site can be reached over a rutted dirt road that is impassable when wet. Permission to visit and directions to the site can be obtained at the U.S. Army Corps of Engineers office at the John Martin Dam. Before visiting the site, even local residents should call the office and register in the log book kept there.

Since all of these sites are on public land, visitation is not a problem. Visitors should remember that the petroglyphs are irreplaceable artifactual elements of our heritage that should not be damaged in any way, not even by touching. In the past, irresponsible people have damaged or destroyed some of the glyphs. Those that are still present are here because other viewers have shown appreciation for their value and have not defaced them. We should all show the same consideration for future visitors. Petroglyph sites are outdoor museums and the glyphs should be treated with the same respect as the exhibits in any museum. When at a petroglyph site, we believe visitors should always follow the code of conduct below.

CODE OF CONDUCT
FOR VISITATION TO PETROGLYPH SITES

DO:
- enjoy the petroglyphs in a spirit of respectfulness.
- photograph and sketch the petroglyphs at will.
- stay on marked trails, drive only on roads, and obey signs.
- avoid standing on ledges or climbing in dangerous places.
- report recent site damage to officials, along with any information about vandals.
- remember that laws have been enacted to protect the sites and there are stiff penalties for damaging them.

DON'T:
- walk on, climb on, shoot at, or carve into any petroglyph panel.
- enhance the images with chalk, crayon, or dusting powder.
- make molds or rubbings of, or even touch, petroglyphs.
- start fires near petroglyph panels.
- remove rocks or artifacts from sites.
- remove lichen from rocks to reveal petroglyphs.
- camp or sleep in ruins, or dig in archaeologically sensitive areas.

At the 1991 annual meeting of the American Rock Art Research Association, A.J. Bock and Georgia Lee presented a paper that included site etiquette recommended by Peter Pilles. Our code is based in part on that paper and on suggestions by Al Kane and Phil Garn.

Examples of petroglyphs on public lands defaced by graffiti. Such irresponsible acts destroy the history and heritage of the region in a manner that cannot be reversed. The spray painting and chalking of the petroglyphs and the carved graffiti are all forms of illegal damage.

CHAPTER 11

A
FINAL VIEW

The region described in this book has many beautiful canyons where one might easily expect to encounter John Wayne or Clint Eastwood riding slowly along the trail. Signs of previous occupation, from tepee rings to homestead ruins, are scattered throughout. Most exciting to us are the many interesting petroglyphs. Some have survived for several millennia and will last for several more, if they are treated with the respect they merit. Petroglyphs are artifacts as deserving of preservation as any displayed in our museums, and eventually, with better understanding, they may even tell us much about those who made them.

Several styles of petroglyphs are present in the region, a wide variety that is strikingly shown by two ship petroglyphs. One is a topsail schooner carved in 1886, and the other a "ship," pecked at the end of a 60-foot-long panel of Pecked Abstract glyphs. The ship's grooves seem to be just as ancient as the rest of the panel. The authors hope that further research will help to explain the presence of such an anomalous glyph.

Southeast Colorado has not seen much detailed archaeological research, and the petroglyphs are just becoming known, even to the professional community. Perhaps this book will help stimulate their study, encourage further efforts for their preservation, and at the same time give the reader some examples of what is present.

Modern topsail schooner, dated 1886. Photo by Susan Touchstone.

Ancient-ship-like petroglyph located at right end of long inscription shown at left, and of the same apparent age. Drawing traced from photo.

Sixty-foot-long Pecked Abstract inscription located 18 feet above present ground level, found and chalk-enhanced by Professor Weisendanger in the late 1940s. Photo courtesy of the No Man's Land Historical Museum, Goodwell, OK.

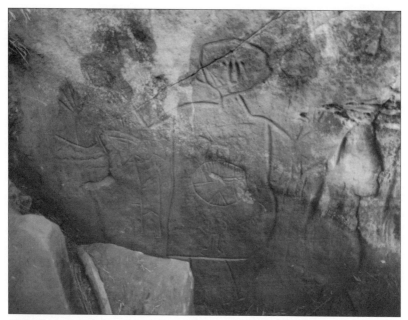

Difficult to classify abraded glyph of older apparent age than the Plains Biographic style. Some think it is a phallic man and others a pregnant woman.

The "Ghostmen of the Picketwire" are large, rubbed, pantaloon-wearing figures of unknown age and origin. Note long-stemmed pipe held by figure at left.

Bent's Old Fort National Historical Site near La Junta, where the early settlement of the american West can be relived, is southeast Colorado's most popular attraction.

Enigmatic petroglyph from Picture Canyon in the Comanche National Grasslands.

Parallel-line petroglyph with two spalled segments held in place. The two replaced pieces were found downhill from the site. A third segment has since been found, but one of the other two spalled pieces has disappeared.

APPENDIX

RECORDING PETROGLYPHS

For readers who may want permanent records of petroglyphs they have seen, the authors provide these recommendations, based on their own recording experiences. Researchers in the past used chalk, crayon, graphite, or aluminum powder to enhance petroglyphs for photography. Latex peels were also taken to prepare reproductions of glyphs, and various types of rubbings and tracings have been made. All of these practices are generally frowned on today. The consensus of opinion of the rock art researchers we have contacted, is that petroglyphs should not be touched by anything including tracing materials or even the fingers. Besides the risk of physical damage, it is believed that surfaces can be chemically contaminated by body oils and salts in a way that may interfere with present and future dating tests. We concur with these restrictions and recommend that petroglyphs not be physically contacted by anything. No form of enhancing materials of any kind, including chalk and crayon, should ever be applied to the rocks.

This does not eliminate recording by other methods. Photography and sketching are acceptable; and it is expected that computerized electronic techniques will be available in the future. Today, we rely principally on photographic recording, and will explain here the specific techniques we employ.

Direct photography of panels using incident light is usually satisfactory, if there is sufficient contrast between petroglyph grooves and background. Glyphs partially lighted by the sun pose a special problem. Three photographs can be taken with exposures set for the lighted area, for the shadowed area, and for an average between them. Alternatively, colleagues can use their bodies or hold coats to shadow the whole glyph, or a portable photographic reflector can be used to illuminate the shadow area. The most difficult situation is photographing heavily patinated panels that have little contrast. We use a bright video light on these glyphs when they are in shadow. The light is held at a low angle to the plane of the panel (about 15°) so that relief lighting is obtained with the grooves shadowed. The light is moved about to maximize the shadowing of grooves that run in different directions.

The video light can be used to assist sketching and to determine the best placements of a flash for relief flash photography. We have found another use for the video light method. Rather than enhancing the glyphs themselves, we return to a site to enhance a previously made photograph of a panel by drawing on the photo with a pen. This requires the use of the video light, as described, to determine the actual location of difficult-to-see grooves. This method has advantages for less artistically talented recorders in that the photo can serve as a guide for drawing the glyph. A tracing can also be made later from the drawing on the photo. Examples of several recording techniques are shown on the following pages. As can be seen from the illustrations, the panel chosen for the comparisons is such a heavily patinated example that photography alone does not yield an acceptable record of the glyph, and some form of sketching is required. In most cases, however, photographs will be satisfactory mementos for visitors.

We normally take black and white photographs for publication and color slides for auditorium presentations. Higher speed films (ASA 200 or 400) work best with the slower lenses on today's zoom cameras, because in exploration work most photos are taken hand-held, and a moderately fast shutter speed is desired. A zoom lens (e.g. 28–105 mm) is very useful for taking both full panels and individual glyphs. When taking archaeoastronomical sequences (e.g. the movement of a shadow across a petroglyph), it is best to set the lens stop for a reading taken in the lighted area. Pictographs are best recorded on color film. Sunlight glaring off a panel is a problem and the use of a polarizing filter can be a valuable aid in reducing the glare. It is also desirable to include a scale reference and a color scale in photographs for serious professional work.

D

Heavily varnished Pecked Abstract panel recorded by various techniques, **Plate I.**
A: *Photo taken in unfavorable lighting conditions by Susan Touchstone.*
B: *Photo taken under favorable lighting conditions by Susan Touchstone.*
C: *Low-contrast print of B with petroglyphs enhanced on the photo on-site by Bill McGlone, using a black pen.*
D: *Tracing of the enhanced petroglyphs on* **C.**
E: *Photo by Susan Touchstone showing use of video light to reveal details of petroglyphs.*

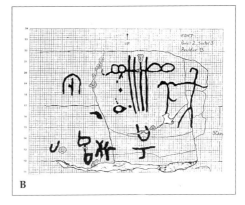

*Heavily varnished Pecked Abstract panel recorded by various techniques, **Plate II.***
A: *Photo of panel with peck marks enhanced on the rock by Ted Barker in 1989 using aluminum powder. This is a practice no longer considered acceptable for recording petroglyphs.*
B: *On-site sketch of panel by Peter Faris.*
C: *Ted Barker (center) making a tracing on mylar of detail of panel. AlmaBarker (left), Bill McGlone (right center), and Peter Faris (right). Photo by Susan Touchstone.*
D: *Tracing of detail on mylar by Don Vickroy. Many recorders object to this method because it requires physical contact with the rock by a foreign material. Others believe the risk is acceptable.*

BIBLIOGRAPHY AND SUGGESTED READING

Campbell, Robert G. 1969. *Prehistoric Panhandle Culture of the Chaquaqua Plateau of Southeast Colorado.* Unpublished doctoral dissertation, U. of Colo.

Dorn, Ronald I., William R. McGlone, and Phillip M. Leonard. 1990. Age Determination of Petroglyphs in Southeast Colorado. *Southwestern Lore* 56 (2): 21–36.

Etter, Jim. 1984. Coronado's Compass: An Oklahoma Puzzle. *Sunday Oklahoman,* Oklahoma City, OK. Aug. 26, pp 1A, 12A.

Grant, Campbell. 1967. *Rock Art of the American Indian.*

Gunnerson, James H. 1989. *Apishipa Canyon Archaeology: Excavations at the Cramer, Snake, Blakeslee and Nearby Sites.* Reprints in Archaeology # 41. Lincoln: J & L Reprint.

Heizer, Robert and Martin Baumhoff. 1962. *Prehistoric Rock Art of Nevada and Eastern California.*

Keyser, James D. 1992. *Indian Rock Art of the Columbian Plateau.*

Loendorf, Lawrence L. 1989. *Nine Rock Art Sites in the Pinon Canyon Maneuver Site, Southeastern Colorado.* Dept. of Anthropology, U. of N. Dakota Contribution 248.

Loendorf, Lawrence L. and D.D. Kuehn. 1991. *1989 Rock Art Research, Pinon Canyon Maneuver Site, Southeastern Colorado.* Dept. of Anthropology, U. of N. Dakota Contribution 258.

Martineau, LaVan. 1973. *The Rocks Begin to Speak.*

McGlone, William R. and Phillip M. Leonard. 1986. *Ancient Celtic America.*

McGlone, William R. and Phillip M. Leonard, James L. Guthrie, Rollin W. Gillespie, and James P. Whittall, Jr. 1993. *Ancient American Inscriptions: Plow Marks or History?*

Mails, Thomas E. 1972. *The Mystic Warriors of the Plains.*

Patterson, Carol. 1985. Deciphering American Indian Pictography. *Epigraphic Society Occasional Publications* 13, # 323.

Renaud, E. B. 1936. *Pictographs and Petroglyphs of the High Western Plains.* The Archaeological Survey of the High Western Plains, U. of Denver.

Sanders, Jerry. 1979. Picasso of the Purgatoire. *Ford Times* 72(9): 60–64.

Winnett, Fred V. and G. Lancaster Harding. 1978. *Inscriptions From Fifty Safaitic Cairns.*

THE AUTHORS

Bill McGlone is a retired engineer who has photographed petroglyphs in 36 states. He has been studying the possibility of pre-Columbian Old World inscriptions in America since 1980.

Ted Barker is a rancher who has lived all his life in southeast Colorado. He has long been interested in its history and has studied the petroglyphs there for the past 15 years.

Phil Leonard has worked in medical and serpentological research and is now employed by the Utah National Guard as the Health Systems Specialist. He has long been interested in linguistic research, with a special emphasis on possible ancient Old World inscriptions in America.

McGlone and Leonard wrote *Ancient Celtic America* in 1986 to present many of the claims that have been made for ancient Old World inscriptions in America. The book is now out of print but is available in local libraries. In 1993, they were part of a team who published *Ancient American Inscriptions: Plow Marks or History?*, which describes both sides of the controversy over American Epigraphy and suggests means for ending it. The book is available from the publisher, Early Sites Research Society, P.O. Box 303, Sutton, MA 01590. (ISBN: 884810-00-4). Both books deal with inscriptions in the southeast Colorado region. Ted Barker has been deeply involved in the research for both volumes.

The present authors have extensively explored the southeast Colorado region, and they assembled most of the material for this book during their study of potential epigraphic inscriptions there.

INDEX

Colorado, Southeast Colorado, Oklahoma, and Oklahoma Panhandle are not indexed because of the frequency with which they occur throughout the book.